Art Nouveau
Jewelry Designs

COLORING BOOK

Carol Schmidt

Dover Publications, Inc.
Mineola, New York

Inspired by the flowing, natural forms characteristic of the Art Nouveau movement, these 31 plates of intricate jewelry designs feature precise renderings of pendants, combs, rings, brooches, earrings, and handbags. The exquisitely detailed accessories in this beautiful collection are adorned with floral motifs, butterflies, birds, and a variety of fanciful creatures. This coloring book is perfect for the advanced colorist and for anyone with an interest in Art Nouveau and decorative jewelry. Plus, the pages are perforated and printed on one side only for easy removal and display.

Copyright

Copyright © 2017 by Carol Schmidt
All rights reserved.

Bibliographical Note

Art Nouveau Jewelry Designs Coloring Book is a new work,
first published by Dover Publications, Inc., in 2017.

International Standard Book Number

ISBN-13: 978-0-486-81224-3
ISBN-10: 0-486-81224-3

Manufactured in the United States by LSC Communications
81224302   2017
www.doverpublications.com

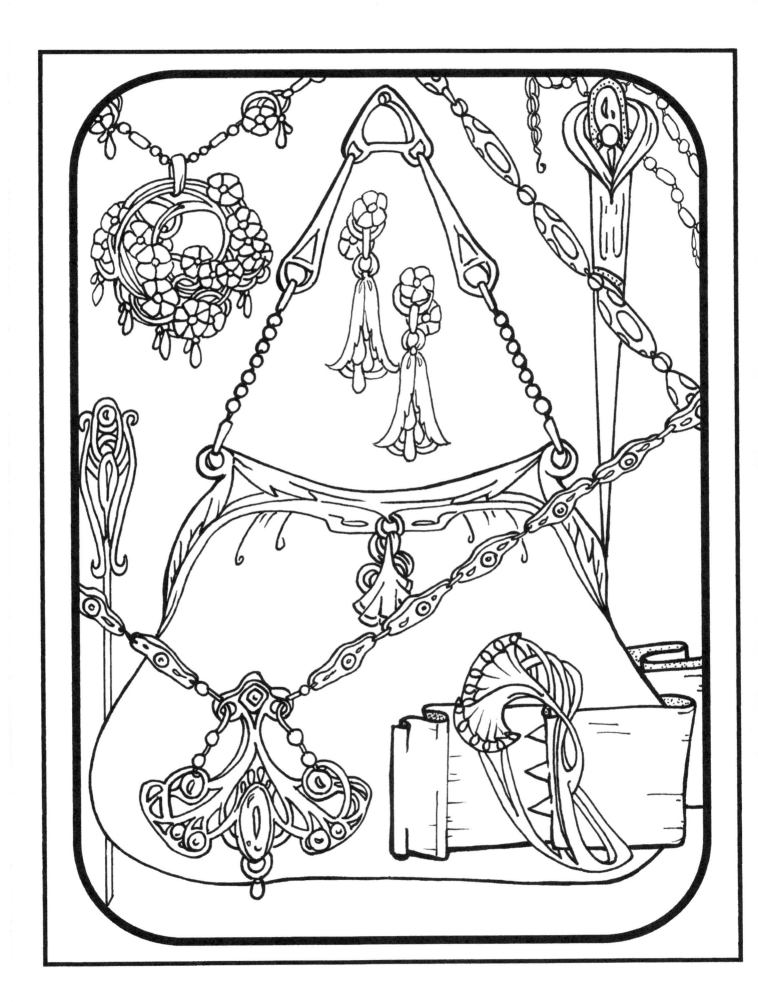

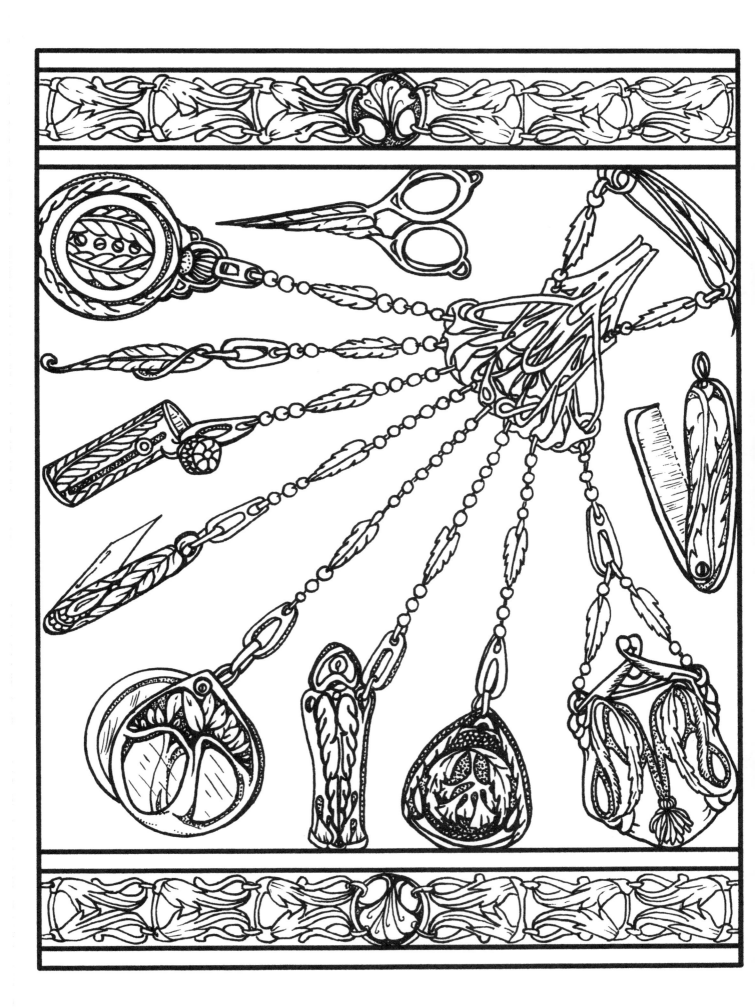

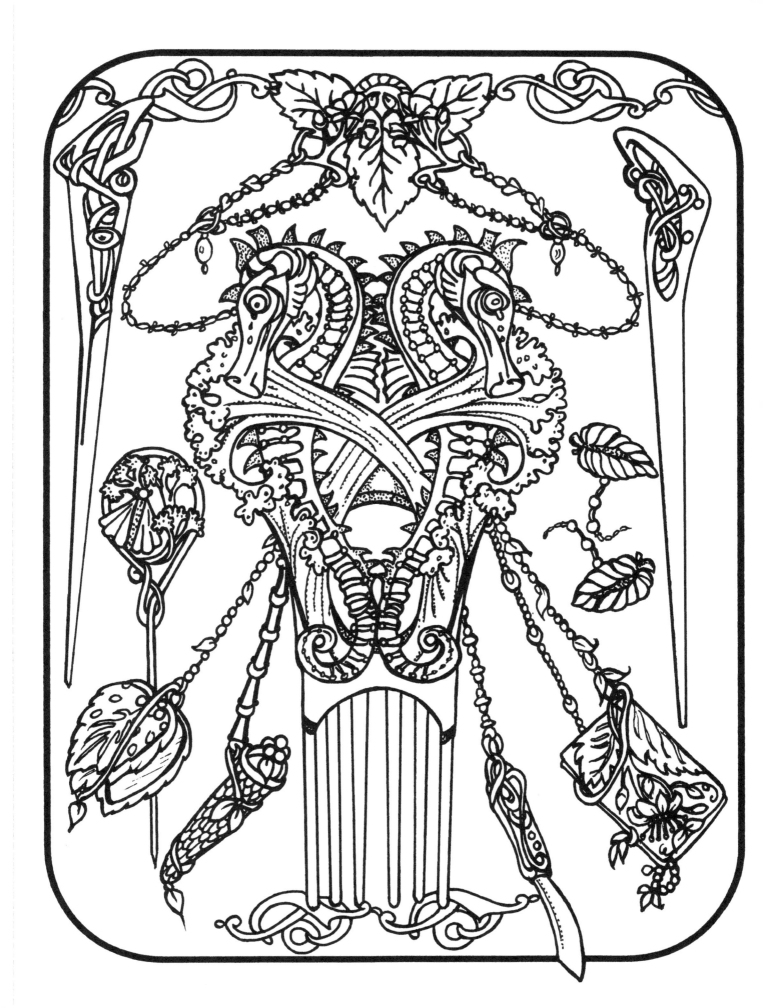

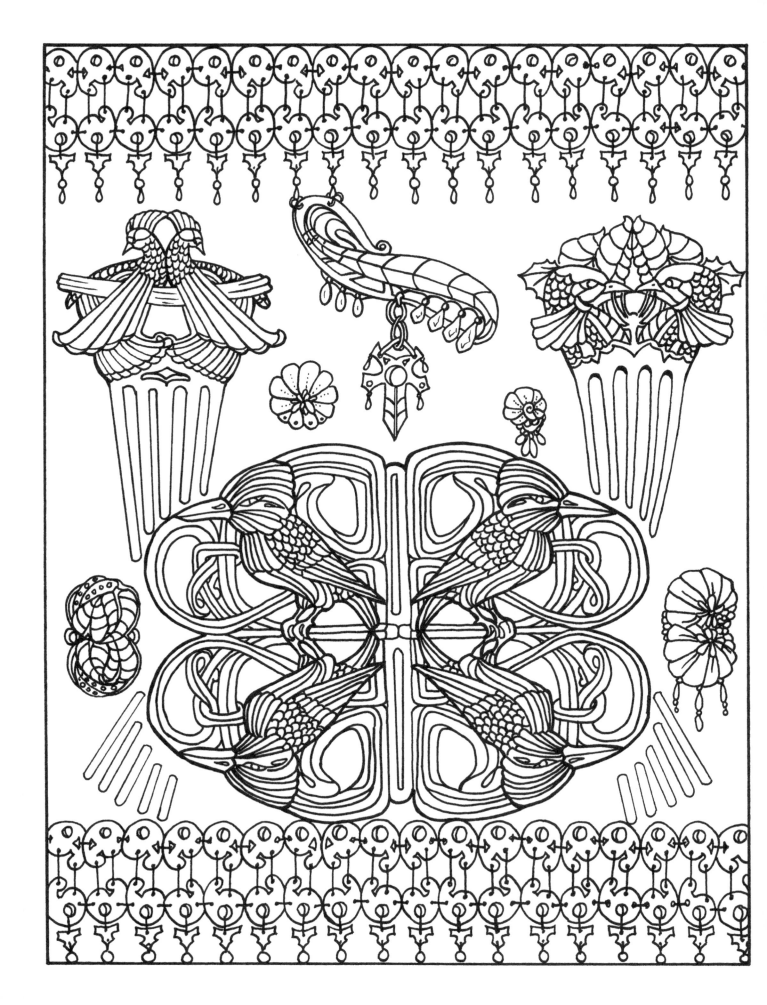